MW00974601

"No man ever loved like Jesus. He taught the blind to see and the dumb to speak. He died on the cross to save us. He bore our sins. And now God says, 'Because He did, I can forgive you.'"
  —Billy Graham

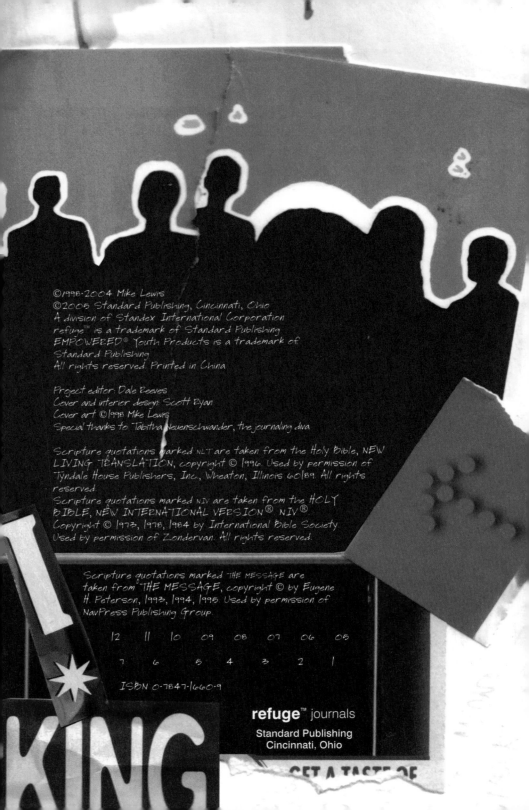

Project editor: Dale Reeves
Cover and interior design: Scott Ryan
Cover art ©1998 Mike Lewis
Special thanks to Tabitha Neuenschwander, the journaling diva

12   11   10   09   08   07   06   05

7   6   5   4   3   2   1

ISBN 0-7847-1660-9

refuge™ journals
Standard Publishing
Cincinnati, Ohio

GET A TASTE OF

KING

"Christ is more of an Artist than the artists; he works in the living spirit and the living flesh; he makes men instead of statues."

—Vincent Van Gogh

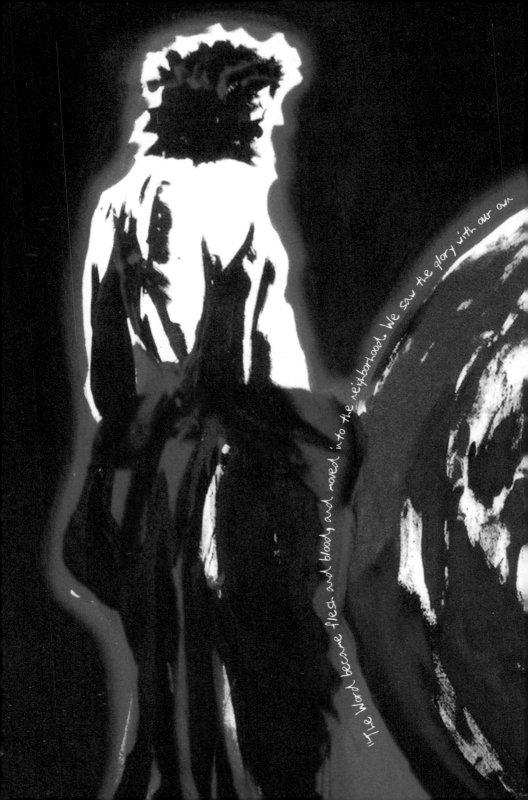

"The Word became flesh and blood, and moved into the neighborhood. We saw the glory with our own eyes, the one-of-a-kind glory, like Father, like Son . . . "—John 1:14, THE MESSAGE

"When God would make His name known to mankind, He could find no better word than 'I AM.' 'I am that I am,' says God, 'I change not.' Everyone and everything else measures from that fixed point."
—A. W. Tozer

"I am the way and the truth Father except through me."
-John 14:6, NIV

and the life. No one comes to the

LUKE 4: 18, 19, NIV

18"The Spirit of the Lord is on me,
    because he has anointed me
    to preach good news to the poor.
He has sent me to proclaim freedom
    for the prisoners
    and recovery of sight for the blind,
to release the oppressed,
19   to proclaim the year of the Lord's
    favor."

w how to express

ound

g-
hall
eas
ice,

s

are

I am the way

"I am the resurrection and the life.
He who believes in me will live, even though he dies."
—John 11:25, NIV

"The Revelation of God is not a book or a doctrine, but a living Person."
—Emil Brunner

"We are all pencils in the hand of a writing God, who is sending love letters to the world."
—Agnes Gonxha Bojaxhiu (Mother Teresa)

"The glory of God is a living man; and the life of man consists in beholding God."
    —Irenaeus

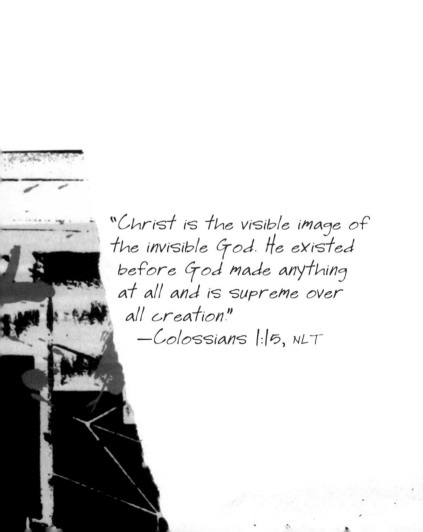

"Christ is the visible image of the invisible God. He existed before God made anything at all and is supreme over all creation."

—Colossians 1:15, NLT

"At the name of Jesus every knee will bow, in heaven and on earth and under the earth, and every tongue will confess that Jesus Christ is Lord, to the glory of God the Father."
—Philippians 2:10, 11, NLT

"We all carry the nails around in our pockets."
—Martin Luther

"You say that I am a king, and you are right. I was born for that purpose. And I came to bring truth to the world. All who love the truth recognize that what I say is true."
—John 18:37, NLT

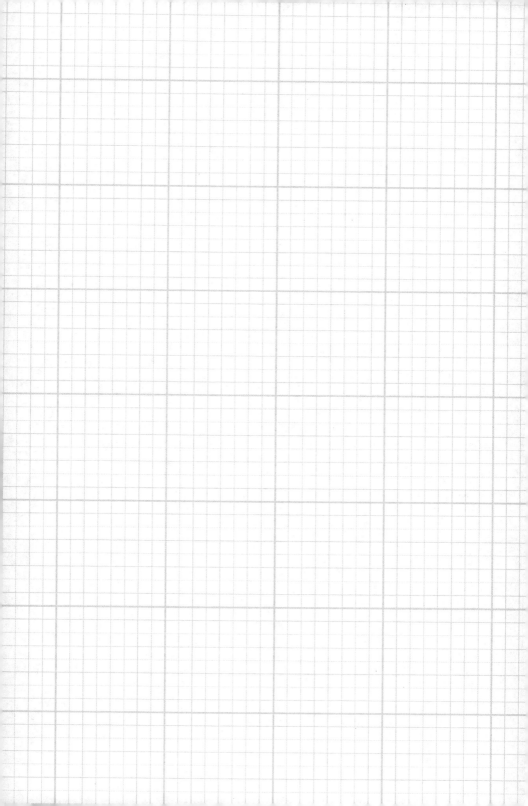

"Father, forgive them,
for they do not know
what they are doing."
—Luke 23:34, NIV

"Who do you say I am?
—Matthew 16:15, NLT

"Nails were not enough to hold God-and-man, nailed and fastened on the Cross, had not love held Him there."
—Catherine of Siena

" If you find the godless world is hating you,
remember it got its start hating me."
—John 15:18, THE MESSAGE

"Jesus Christ is the end of all, and the centre to which all tends. Whoever knows Him knows the reason of everything." —Blaise Pascal

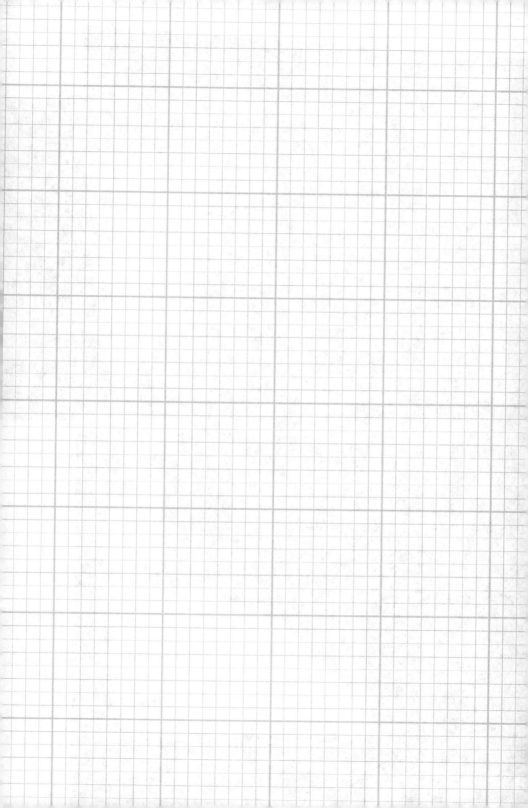

"He canceled the record that contained the charges against us. He took it and destroyed it by nailing it to Christ's cross."

—Colossians 2:14, NLT

"Forgiveness breaks the chain of causality because he who forgives you—out of love—takes upon himself the consequences of what you have done. Forgiveness, therefore, always entails a sacrifice."
        —Dag Hammarskjold

"I am the bread of life. No one who comes to me will ever be hungry again. Those who believe in me will never thirst."
—John 6:35, NLT

" It is the creative potential itself in human
beings that is the image of God."
—Mary Daly

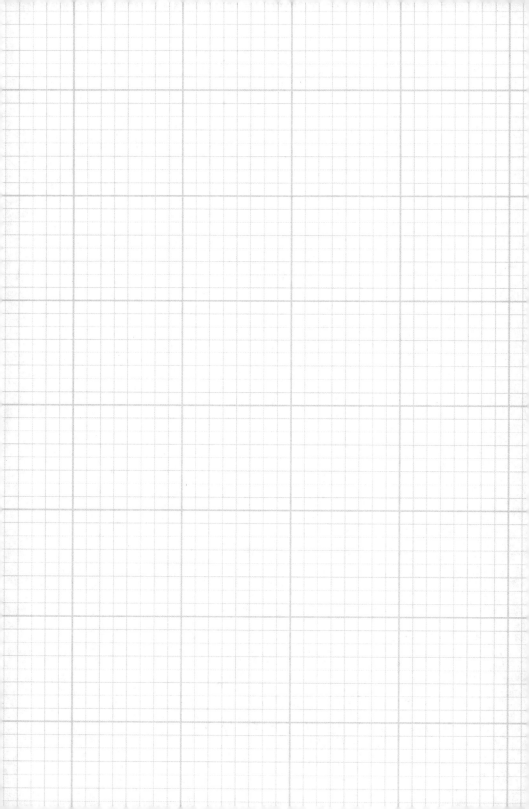

"The color of the object illuminated partakes of the color of that which illuminates it."
—Leonardo da Vinci

"I am the good shepherd; I know my own sheep, and they know me, just as my Father knows me and I know the Father. And I lay down my life for the sheep."
—John 10:14, 15, NLT

"I am the light of the world. Whoever follows me will never walk in darkness, but will have the light of life." —John 8:12, NIV

"Believe in the light while there is still time; then you will become children of the light."
—John 12:36, NLT

Mike Lewis, who is known as the Jesus Painter, paints large portraits of Christ at about 120 events per year. He studied fine arts at Harding University. Mike and his wife reside in Oveido, Florida. His art is featured on the cover, pages 1, 4-5, 20-21, 42-43, 48, 84-85, and 103 of this journal.

To enjoy more of Mike's artwork, visit his Web site at www.jesuspainter.com.